# How to Argue with a Cat

# How to Argue with a Cat

*A Human's Guide to the Art of Persuasion*

JAY HEINRICHS

Illustrated by Natalie Palmer-Sutton

RODALE.

Copyright © 2018 by Jay Heinrichs
Illustrations © 2018 by Natalie Palmer-Sutton

All rights reserved.
Published in the United States by Rodale Books,
an imprint of the Crown Publishing Group, a division of
Penguin Random House LLC, New York.
crownpublishing.com
rodalebooks.com

RODALE and the Plant colophon are registered
trademarks of Penguin Random House LLC.

Originally published in hardcover in
Great Britain by Penguin Books, a division of
Penguin Random House LLC, London, in 2018.

Library of Congress Cataloging-in-Publication Data is available.

ISBN 978-1-63565-274-1
Ebook ISBN 978-1-63565-275-8

Printed in the United States of America

*Cover illustration by Natalie Palmer-Sutton*

7th Printing
First American Edition

*For Charlie, Maturin and Killick, and in memory of dear Aubrey and Percy*

"Dear cat, your ears are flipped inside out, so I know you're not listening to a word I'm not saying."

Jarod Kintz

# Contents

# CONTENTS

# How to Argue with a Cat

# Introduction

"They're exactly like us minus our useless mental
power and thumbs."

—Bob Tarte

When people asked me for a beginner's guide to the art of
persuasion, I thought, *Cats*. Then I thought, *Terrible idea*.
Persuading people is hard. Persuading cats? Much, much
harder, because they rank among the world's top negotiators. They are masters in the dark art of persuasion.

Being a lover of cats myself, I have personal experience
of arguing with them. Although I have written a bestselling book on persuasion, I still lose most of the arguments I have with my two cats, Maturin and Killick.

Then something happened that made me change my
mind. I was giving a persuasion workshop at an advertising agency in London. During a break to check my emails
I borrowed the office of the art director, Natalie Palmer-Sutton. Her walls were covered with brilliant cat art. The
pictures looked as if Natalie had peered right past her
cats' pretty faces and into their devious little souls. If she
could do that, I thought, I just might be up to the challenge. Maybe I could uncover their cunning tricks to
charm and convince. It would be worth the effort. If you
could learn to persuade a cat, then any human—friend,

loved one, boss, even a teenager, for crying out loud—
would bow to your magic.

I begged Natalie to team up with me. We would try to
make people laugh while teaching them the best secrets
for persuading anyone. Including a cat. This book is the
result.

"Wait," says a non-cat person. *"Cats don't talk."*

Sure they do. They purr. They meow. We know one who
makes weird happy grunting noises when he eats. Admittedly, half the time you don't know exactly what cats are
talking about. But whose fault is that? Besides, half the time
we don't know what *humans* are talking about. Cats and
people alike frequently talk nonsense. Both often behave
illogically. But if you know a few tricks, you can get along
with even the most stubborn and senseless cat or human.

This is the theory behind rhetoric, the art of persuasion. Invented almost 3,000 years ago by ingenious Greeks,
rhetoric was studied by such luminaries as the philosopher
Aristotle. He wrote the classic book on the subject—after
he finished his famous one on logic. Aristotle realized
that, while logic is excellent and noble, and a first-rate way
to make a friend look like a drooling idiot, a perfectly
logical argument fails to persuade most of the time. Aristotle and the rhetoricians who came after him discovered
that other factors persuade people better than logic,
namely, our emotions, our identities, and the people we
hang around with. This book, based on many years of
studying rhetoric—and of observing cats, those masters of
the art—will show you how to use these factors to persuade humans (and cats).

Just keep in mind that cats are not quite the suckers you and I are. Being more cautious and skeptical, they tend to be wiser than humans, especially when it comes to inter-species relations. Still, cats are no more logical than humans. The same rhetorical tricks can work for both. Learning to argue with cats will not only improve your relationships with cats, it will help you get along with humans.

Cat persuasion techniques can also protect you against the tricks pulled on you by marketers, politicians, and dodgy sorts of all stripes. Like these people, cats are skilled manipulators who can talk you into just about anything with scarcely a word. They can get you to drop whatever you're doing and play with them. They can make you serve their dinner way ahead of schedule. They can get you to sit down right this instant and provide a lap.

On the other hand, try getting a cat to do what *you* want.

While it's hard, persuading a cat is possible. And after that, persuading humans becomes a breeze. You just need to learn the persuasion skills in this book. We'll teach you how to:

- Hold an intelligent conversation—one of the few things easier to do with a cat than a human.

- Argue logically, even if your opponent is hairy and irrational.

- Hack up a fallacy (the hairball of logic).

- Make your body do the talking. (Cats are very good at this.)

- Master decorum, the art of fitting in with cats, venture capitalists or humans.

- Learn the wisdom of predator timing and pounce at the right moment.

- Get someone to do something, or stop doing it.

- Earn any creature's respect and loyalty.

The tools to accomplish these feats come from Aristotle and the other masters in the art of persuasion. We hope this book makes the art easy to practice. The tools in here are simple, even if cats aren't. Once you get comfortable with them, you might consider learning more about rhetoric in *Thank You for Arguing*.

Meanwhile, relax. An argument doesn't have to lead to spitting and scratching. Remember, an agreeable lap goes a long way. And, as the next chapter shows, resolving a disagreement starts by simply being agreeable.

Jay Heinrichs

# When in doubt, keep a straight face.

Cats rarely change their expression.
That's one reason they look so dignified.
It also helps them hide their ploys.

# 1. Practice Agreeability: The Brilliant Purr

*Turn a disagreement into a beautiful relationship*

"To err is human, to purr is feline."
—Robert Byrne

The first thing every cat knows, and you should know too, is that an argument is not a fight. In a fight, you try to *win*. You want to dominate the other person and make him admit defeat. The loser in a fight is never very happy about it.

In an argument, you try to *win over* the other creature. You get your opponent to agree on a solution, or to make a choice. While both a fight and an argument start with a disagreement, only an argument can make both sides happy. How? By reaching an agreement that benefits both of you. In the best kind of argument, both sides think they won.

A cat knows the difference by instinct. When she sinks her teeth into you, she means to fight. It's a play-fight maybe, but still fighting. She is not interested in a useful conversation. Her goal is to win the fight.

Same thing when a little boy sinks his teeth into his sister. This probably isn't a play-fight. He probably feels angry. Still, his goal is the same as the cat's. He wants to beat his sister in a fight.

Most adults don't bite each other. Not much, anyway. Instead, they fight by trying to score points off each other. They often treat a disagreement as a kind of debate. It's as if they think an invisible panel will be holding up score cards at the end, judging who won the most points in the debate.

Or an adult will point out how the disagreement proves what a jerk the other person is. Or she'll point out her opponent's past idiotic opinions and mistakes. In each case, she is not arguing. She's fighting. Trying to win. From a persuasion standpoint, her behavior works about as well as biting does, though it's maybe a little less painful.

So is there a way to turn a disagreement into something positive? Yes. By arguing. An argument is not about domination. It's about getting another person to make a choice or take an action that you want.

A cat who bites means to fight. But a cat who gently claws your leg is making an argument: *Pay me attention. I want food/play/love/access to high places.* (Every cat was a monkey in his past life.)

The leg-clawing offers the perfect opening to an intelligent dialogue, where you can share points of view and develop a mutually satisfying conclusion.

Jay: Want to get up on the highest bookshelf?
    The one you can never get down from?
Killick: [*Claws a little more insistently.*]
Jay: How about my shoulder? [*Picks up the cat.*]

Killick: [*Balances precariously on Jay's shoulder, looking meaningfully at the highest shelf.*]
Jay: Tell you what. We'll go check the bird feeder out the window and imagine eating the sparrows.
Killick: [*Aims Jay towards the window.*]

This is the perfect argument. Killick enjoys the high vantage point, and Jay has an excuse to skip a chore. An argument starts with a disagreement and ends up with a choice that both sides can live with.

A fight, on the other hand, usually comes with anger. While an argument can also start with somebody getting angry, the whole point is to settle something. To make a mutual choice.

Jay: Who knocked over the lamp?
Killick: [*Looks thoughtfully into the distance.*]
Jay: Not you? Really? Do you think your habit of jumping on to tables might have had something to do with it?
Killick: [*Sits in a neutral corner.*]
Jay: So if I get a bigger lamp, there won't be any room left on the table for you.
Killick: [*Grooms, perfectly satisfied with the outcome.*]

Humans tend to get defensive at moments like this, claiming innocence instead of fixing the problem.

Jay: Who knocked over the lamp?
Child: Not me!

We need to learn from cats. Air your disagreements with the aim of finding solutions.

One way to take the anger out is to propose a choice. Aristotle called this kind of conversation a **deliberative argument**. Deliberation has to do with choices. Here's the important thing about presenting these choices: You have to show how they benefit your audience. (Aristotle called this tool the **advantageous**. It works great on humans but isn't necessary for cats. They already know what's to their advantage.)

Suppose you want to go to a concert on Saturday. Your partner doesn't want to. He looks tired. Instead of saying, "Come on, we never go out enough!," try offering a choice.

> You: I just thought the concert would be amazing. It's the one kind of music we agree on. But if you're too tired to go out, we could just invite the Smiths over. They're very restful people.
>
> Partner: Restful? You mean boring.
>
> You: You're right. Way too boring. I'll get us concert tickets.

Again, this may not work, and you'll need to master the other tools in this book. But the advantageous ploy sounds a lot less whiny than the usual argument.

Still, what about Killick, our lamp-knocking cat? Jay may have to make the choice himself. (Actually, that's sort of what you did with the concert. Cats and partners aren't that terribly different, after all.) Jay can move the table to where it will never catch the sunlight. Or he can buy a bigger lamp. Or he could try to get Killick to promise never to knock the lamp over again.

That last choice probably won't work. A human may make such a promise without being sure he can actually keep it. But a cat knows better.

Okay, but what if your opponent continues to bite your leg? Or, if he isn't the biting type, what if he just tells you you're wrong and that you're a total jerk? In other words, what if you want to argue with an opponent who just wants to fight? Here are several tools you can use to keep things cool and turn a fight into an argument.

## 1. Be agreeable

Here is one of the many ways that cats are wiser than people: When a human disagrees with another human, each usually tries to get the other to admit he's wrong. When a cat disagrees with a human, on the other hand, she almost always tries to get what she wants. Cats also understand that one of the best ways to persuade people is to be agreeable. This is a skill that even humans can learn. Agreeability can lead to happier relationships, successful careers and a more persuasive life.

Even if you disagree with someone, or your opponent attacks you personally, nod your head and listen. Don't get angry. And don't push back against any of his points. Hold your fire.

You often see cats acting agreeably.

Natalie: I can't believe you napped on my new dress!
Charlie: [*Looks at Natalie and listens politely.*]

Natalie: It will take forever to get all the hair out! And I'm supposed to be at dinner in half an hour!

Charlie: [*Blinks.*]

Natalie: What am I going to do with you?

Charlie: [*Does a slow-blink, letting slide the stupidity of Natalie's question.*]

Natalie: Well, maybe I can use a sticky roller on it.

Charlie: [*Stretches. Problem solved.*]

## 2. Say "Yes, and . . ."

If you have ever taken an improv class, you'll know this method. You work with fellow comedians as a team. When someone says something, you don't argue against it. Instead, you add to it, fleshing out what the other person said. You do this by saying "Yes, and . . ." This is one of those rare things humans do better than cats.

Of course, cats don't need to say "Yes, and . . ." Instead, they have expressive tails. A gentle thump or wag will disarm your average human opponent.

Because we don't have tails, we have to practice other methods, like improv, to disarm our human opponents.

Manager: I looked at your proposal for a dance theme at the office party, and I think we need to go in another direction. Instead of "Fist Pump" (what kind of theme is "Fist Pump"?), I think we should call the dance "Under the Sea." Everybody loved *Little Mermaid*.

You: "Under the Sea." Sure, an aquatic theme. We can call it "Fin Pump."

12

Manager: Huh? What's a fin pump?
You: Right, good point. And it's better to just call it plain
 "Fist Pump."


While this may not work, at least you will have confused the boss for a while. Which is satisfying. A cat can do this just by staring at you or by stretching against your leg. This makes you wonder whether she really got your message—or whether she has a mysterious message of her own.


## 3. Groom your opponent

A cat can take the tension out by licking her opponent. In most cases, humans probably should not do this. Licking an angry person will probably not calm him down. But a small dose of flattery might work.

Father: I want to know who ate the last of the cookies.
Teen: Well . . . Wow.
Father: Well?
Teen: Sorry, I was distracted by your shoes. Those are
 really cool shoes!
Father: We're not here to talk about my shoes! We're here
 to talk about my cook– I mean, the family . . . You
 know what I mean!


The teen may still be in trouble. And the father may see right past her flattery. But Dad will also shine his shoes tonight, thinking maybe his kid isn't so bad after all. Though she shouldn't have eaten those cookies.

CAT WISDOM

# You're always welcome.

The cat secret to agreeability: Walk around as if the
world adores you. The whole world becomes your lap.
Go lie in it.

# 2. Pounce Like a Predator: The Art of Stalking

*Learn persuasion's timing secret*

"Did St. Francis preach to the birds? Whatever for?
If he really liked birds he would have done better to
preach to the cats."

—Rebecca West

What does waiting have to do with argument? A lot. Too often in a dispute we chase after arguments like silly dogs. We trip over each other, barking and getting angry. We nip at each other without pinning any argument down. We attack each other and lose our way and pretty much look like idiots.

Instead we should argue like a real predator, such as a cat.

This will take some work and patience because humans lack an important physical trait. Unlike cats, we have eyes that see all over the place. Our peripheral vision constantly distracts us. Laugh all you want at those videos that show cats' heads bobbing in unison. They are behaving like predators. A predator tracks its prey with its whole body. Cats are like police who look wherever their pistol is pointing, aiming their bodies the way they aim their guns.

Remember this, and you'll understand an important thing about argument: *Everything a cat sees looks like a target.*

In an argument—with human or cat—we need to practice the same laser focus. When you find yourself in a disagreement, set your target. Decide what your goal is—what you want to aim at achieving.

Rhetoric teaches three basic goals of persuasion. They range from easy to hard.

## 1. Change the mood

This is the easiest goal to achieve. If your opponent is a bit grouchy, then a favorite song or a glass of wine or a snoutful of catnip will often do the job. If your opponent is angry, you may just want to wait until the mood passes. Or you can sympathize, say you feel bad about what happened and offer to fix the problem. With a cat, you can usually skip the apology and go straight to fixing the problem. That's because a cat is more sensible. One who finds a strange cat in her litter box will quickly calm down if you remove the intruder. (That second cat might resent being removed in the middle of doing his business, but that's a different problem.)

We'll get to other ways to handle emotions in a later chapter. Meanwhile, just know that changing the mood in the room can be one big goal of an argument. You're not trying to win anything. You don't want to dominate your opponent and prove you're the alpha, just put your opponent in a happy, calm state.

But suppose you want to get something more out of the

argument. Suppose you want to change your opponent's mind about something. It's still good to work on her mood first. Now you're ready for goal number 2.

## 2. Change his mind

This is much more difficult than changing the mood. It is fairly easy to cheer up a grouchy grandmother. Getting her to think differently about hip-hop? Probably a lot harder. Getting someone excited about an election: quite possible. Getting him to change his mind and vote for your favorite candidate: much harder.

Naturally, this is true of cats as well. Try convincing a cat who grew up without dogs that dogs are man's best friend. Now try convincing the same cat that she should make friends with a dog.

Yes, it's possible. But you're probably not going to achieve that goal in a single argument. In this book you'll find a number of tools that will help change someone's mind. Still, it takes practice.

But there's an even more challenging goal.

## 3. Change his willingness to do something

You can get an apathetic older brother excited about the election. Maybe you can change his mind about a candidate. Now try getting him to go to the polls on election day and actually vote for that candidate. If you succeed, you win the grand prize of persuasion. You have persuaded someone to take an action.

Getting someone to *stop* taking an action can be just as hard. Most cats reasonably expect that the kitchen counter is part of their territory. A roasted chicken cooling on top of that counter lies within cat territory. Therefore, it's reasonable to assume that the chicken is there for the cat. (And possibly for humans as well, if the cat is feeling generous.) You can understand why it's hard to keep a cat from jumping on top of the counter. Especially if you insist on putting chicken on it.

First, you have to change the cat's mood. You could get him to decide he's not hungry. A treat might do the job. Or you could get him to fear the counter—a crude and unpleasant form of persuasion we do not recommend. Or you could put the chicken into the refrigerator and run to get a favorite toy. Not all cats are so easily distracted, but yours might be.

Next, you change the cat's mind. Get him to decide he doesn't like chicken. Good luck with that. Maybe you could coat something disgusting over the chicken—peanut butter?—but that might change your own mind about eating chicken.

Sometimes you can go straight toward changing the action. To get someone to vote, you can drive him to the polls and hope for the best. To get a cat to stop jumping up on the counter, you can catch him and place him gently on the floor. Over and over again.

Hey, we didn't say persuasion was always easy.

But none of these three goals—mood, mind, action—has to do with winning. None of these goals has you getting distracted with scoring points or pointing out logical fallacies or making your opponent look like an idiot. Instead, you focus on your target—again, mood, mind or action—and you aim everything at it. You're arguing like a predator.

Okay, so you know how to set your goal. You're not going to win an argument on points. You're not going to try to pin your opponent down (unless you're play-fighting and your claws are retracted). Before you get to the actual arguing part, you need another predator skill: timing.

The secret of persuasion is just like the secret of comedy. It's timing. And timing in persuasion takes an extra amount of patience. After setting your goal, effective persuasion depends on waiting for the right moment.

### Catch the bald guy

In rhetoric, this art of waiting for the perfect moment is called **kairos** (KI-ros). Someone skilled at kairos, such as a cat, not only knows how to wait. She also knows exactly the right moment to act, to seize the occasion, letting no temporary lap go un-sat-upon and no bug unchased.

Much of persuasion depends on kairos. Someone who is not ready to be persuaded won't be ready until her mood changes. For instance, never ask someone to cook you dinner while he is cleaning a toilet. (Only cats and dogs can keep their appetite around toilets.) Never ask a favor when someone is angry. And never ever, under any circumstances, say, "Calm down." That just ruins every occasion.

Practice timing in any office meeting by speaking last. Wait until people want to hear from you.

When you're in a one-on-one argument, nod your head and say something like, "This is what I'm hearing from you." Repeat those words, then say what you like about what you've heard. Only then show where you disagree.

In the dinner-table political argument, the sister should try to look like a neutral party until the brother finally shuts up. If he shows no signs of quitting, she should interrupt by saying, "That makes a lot of sense, but let's be sure I understand you." Then, when she's ready, she states the other side.

(By the way, we're talking about the timing of human arguments here. When arguing with a cat, don't wait for the cat to finish talking. She is probably smart enough not to talk at all. With a cat argument, wait until the cat wants something. Then try to bargain. This works with kids as well.)

The three greatest words in argument: *Wait for it.*

Hang back until you're ready, or your audience is ready, or your opponent has talked himself out, or your lover is in the mood, or your cat needs something.

The Romans thought the art of occasion to be so important, they created a god called Occasio. (That's where we get the word "occasion" from.) Young and fleet, with the body of a runner, Occasio had a hair-loss problem. While he had curly locks over his brow, he was bald as an olive at the back. That's because an opportunity ages fast. You have to grab the occasion by the hair before it passes—just as you would with a mouse.

But before you pounce, you must stalk.

## *The wiggle and bob*

Your average adult human is incompetent when it comes to play. This is terribly frustrating to your average cat. The human wastes time making his mostly inedible dinner and talking about work before finally—finally!—taking out the string with a mouse on the end. Excellent! The cat happily chases the mouse, pounces on it, bats it around and follows it all over the place for a good five minutes. This is the warm-up. Humans, please listen: *The chasing part is just the warm-up.* Then comes the serious play: settling down to watch the mouse. And what does the human do? He puts the mouse away!

People, people! Watching a toy *is* playing. It's the best part. A cat who watches a toy isn't bored or tired. She has just entered the entertaining second round—like the second half of that uncatlike sport of football. An intelligent, cooperative human will keep pulling the string around and around. After a good long period of watching, the cat will gather her back legs and wiggle her butt and bob her head, getting a good bead on the prey. Does she necessarily pounce? No! The wiggle and bob are sufficient unto themselves. They are totally fun in their own right, and part of the experience of being a healthy predator. To a cat, stalking is half the pounce. Let us repeat:

Stalking is half the pounce.

Maybe more than half; no one really knows, since cats don't bother to explain the process.

The point is, nearly every cat understands the power and delight of kairos, of choosing just the right occasion to pounce. Being a predator is all about kairos. If cats had spent their first million years of evolution charging around after prey like dogs, cats would have had to form packs like dogs. This would have been a whole lot of bother and would have forced cats to hang out with other cats, some of whom might not be all that likable.

Instead, early on, the wise cats developed the fine art of waiting. They learned to read the patterns of rodents and birds, to let the food come to them. A little bit of sneaking, along with a well-prepared pounce, completes the job. Boom, done. Mission accomplished with a minimum of inefficient and sometimes embarrassing running. Now go take a nap.

## *Await your chance*

Humans have a long way to catch up with this kind of wisdom. Monks and yogis spend decades just learning how to sit still, and even then they don't catch anything worth eating.

Or win many arguments, for that matter.

What does waiting have to do with argument? A lot. To argue like a predator, settle down. Watch and listen.

Pay attention to your prey—that is, your opponent. Then gather your thoughts, wiggle your mind and gain a good perspective on the issue. When you're ready, pounce.

Suppose you're in the meeting where people are trying to choose a theme for the annual office party. People are fighting over one woman's proposal for a "world peace" theme. Someone else proposes an ironic eighties theme with mullets; this produces much eye-rolling. You are sorely tempted to jump in, shout down the lame ideas and propose your own awesome concept of a single-color theme: red. No word, no stupid slogan, just red, though you'd be willing to settle for purple. But you don't say anything. You listen, and you wait until the time is ripe. The other participants talk themselves out, and there's a pause. Time to pounce.

You: Red.
Everybody else: What?
You: Red. Just red. The color. No words.

You have a shot, a real shot, at getting your way. In the cat world, this is called "hunting." To a cat, hunting means waiting; the pounce just tops it off. The real skill lies in being patient.

## Use the right medium

With humans, kairos has dimensions beyond just timing. It's also the art of the *occasion*, which includes place or medium as well as time. The bedroom is a very different place, persuasion-wise, from the kitchen. Bedtime is different from mealtime. Emails, tweets, whispers in the ear, Morse code and skywriting are different media. Each place and medium affects the persuasion.

When you want to persuade someone, choose the right occasion. Cats know this. The point is not just to wait for the right moment to pounce; cat and mouse both have to be in the right place.

Suppose a man wants to take a woman on a date. He could offer to pick her up at 4:00 in the morning, but this is probably bad timing, unless his (and her) idea of a good time is predawn fishing. Instead, he offers to pick her up at 7:00 in the evening. Better timing. Also, a Friday night might work better than a Monday night, but he should check on that as well.

Okay, the man has the date sorted, timing-wise. So he takes her to his favorite bar, where all his drinking buddies hang out.

Um, *possibly* this is a good occasion. But for a first date, not so much.

So instead he takes her to a quiet restaurant. Afterward, he plans a stroll by moonlight beside a nearby lake. She might like that. But even if that's the sort of thing she might do on a first date, the man probably shouldn't propose it until well into dinner, when she's really into him and he has learned that she likes walking and that her shoes aren't killing her. When the time is perfectly right, he proposes the walk. That's kairos. The wait and the pounce, rhetorically speaking.

Then there's medium. A text message works differently

from a Pinterest post. A serenade beneath a window will have a different effect from a proposal with a bullhorn.

Guys can be real boneheads when it comes to this kind of kairos. We have a friend who planned to propose marriage to his girlfriend by taking her rock climbing. He was going to place the ring on a tiny ledge near the top of the route. Imagine: Sweaty and terrified, forty feet above her boyfriend who's holding the rope, she places her shaking hand on a rock, knocks something loose from the ledge and falls. He tightens his grip on the rope, and while she's swinging with her eyes tightly shut, he watches the ring tumble into the distance and in despair he shouts, "Will you marry me?"

Fortunately, we talked him out of this plan. He proposed over dinner and she said yes. Less dramatic, more effective. The right occasion.

## *Match media to senses*

Different media emphasize different aspects of persuasion.

A *picture* is best for conveying an impression of your character. A cat sitting in the window with perfect posture does the same thing.

*Type* does the best job of logical argument. Words that you can see on a page or screen are great for organized thinking. Very few cats can write things down, except for paw prints on the stove. But then, cats rarely use logical argument. While type is great for logic, it's not so good for getting someone to like and trust you. It's also bad for conveying emotion. Humor in a text or email, for instance, rarely goes down well. It may have seemed hilarious when you wrote it, but the readers can't see you make an ironic face. (Cats also don't make ironic faces, which is why their sense of humor tends to go underappreciated.)

The *sound of your voice* can make people respect you, or not. An audience tends to trust a deeper voice that does not soar too much between high and low notes. This does not mean a woman has to talk bass; instead, try to talk in a near-monotone, with pauses for emphasis. Watch George Clooney movies for the perfect monotone. A high voice, on the other hand, can make people want to help you. We instinctively think "baby." Cats already know this. When a cat wants food, he uses baby talk, throwing out an adorable high mew. A cat defending his turf, on the other hand, talks deep and low, like George Clooney.

The best senses for emotion are *touch*, *taste* and *smell*. A cat will tell you that taste and smell also work great for building relationships, and he's probably right. To propose marriage, you really should be there next to the person. Don't send a text or hire a dance troupe to do the job. Don't make a video. Kiss, or, if you prefer, bite gently on the back of the neck. Do some mutual grooming.

# The listening cat catches the mouse.

The early bird can have its worm.
A patient, quiet cat eats better.

# 3. Defuse Anger: The Toilet Argument

*Cool things down with a thing called the future*

> "A cat's rage is beautiful, burning with pure cat flame, all its hair standing up and crackling blue sparks, eyes blazing and sputtering."
> —William S. Burroughs

Cats get angry just as people do, and for pretty much the same reasons. (Though, since most cats don't drive cars, they get angry less often.) Cats and people get angry when:

They're disrespected.
They're disappointed.
They're lied to.
They're denied a Good Thing. (This, to a cat, is the same as being lied to.)
Their territory gets invaded.

Cats, like people, don't like to be laughed at when they're angry. And the very, very worst thing you can do to angry cats or people is tell them to calm down. Telling someone to calm down implies that his anger is his own fault. Anyone who's angry believes that someone else, not him, is to blame. And if he thinks you're to blame, and you're the one telling him to calm down . . . well! Keep a respectful distance from his claws.

So what *do* you do with an angry cat or human? Let's start with a human. Then we'll work our way up to cats.

An argument between people almost always covers one of three topics.

## *Topic: blame*

*"You left it up again!?"*

Your partner left the toilet seat up, and the cat drank out of it again.

When you blame someone for leaving the toilet seat up, what kind of mood are you in? Are you admiring the beauty of the oval lid? Laughing at the thought of sitting down and falling in? Thinking sadly of how so much in life goes down the drain?

Probably not. Most likely, you're doing some fast detective work, quickly deciding on the perpetrator, *and then getting mad* at the jerk. Chances are this isn't the first time he has committed this crime. He's a repeat offender. And you have prosecuted him before. Many times. He is beginning to look like the kind of criminal who cannot be reformed. So the only thing to do at the moment is to yell at him. Take out your frustration.

Not to mention the cat. She has fresh water laid out just for her, clean water in her very own watering place on the floor. So why does she insist on drinking out of the toilet? Your house is full of evildoers.

Now think of your partner. How does he react when you yell at him? He feels defensive. Or he thinks you are overreacting. I mean, you're both dealing with car payments and job stress and meanwhile the Earth is warming and there's terrorism and fake news and global horror everywhere. And you're bothered about a toilet seat?

This kind of stupid, beside-the-point attitude drives you even crazier. So you raise your voice more. Which now makes him angry. Which makes you angrier. And so on.

Meanwhile, the cat is the only grown-up in the room. Actually she is not in the room. She's sensibly hiding under the bed. Loud voices hurt her sensitive ears.

So how is this blame thing working out for you? Blame is a topic that leads to anger. Especially in humans.

## Topic: values

*"A good partner wouldn't leave the toilet seat up!"*

Instead of pointing out your partner's crime, you talk about his character. A good spouse would care about your cat's hygiene and the risk of her drowning in the toilet. Not to mention the likelihood of you falling in yourself.

Values have to do with good and bad, right and wrong— who's right and who's wrong. Being considerate about the toilet seat: good. Being inconsiderate: bad. A spouse who's inconsiderate is a bad spouse. And therefore a bad person. In short, leaving the toilet seat up proves what a complete jerk your partner is. Values are the nuclear option of argument, blowing up any chance of a solution. This is no longer about putting the toilet seat down. It's about an entire sinking relationship.

(And the cat? We'll leave the cat out of this. As it is, she's leaving herself out of the entire conversation.)

So what kind of mood are you in while accusing another person of being rotten to the core? And what kind of mood do you think that puts *him* in?

The problem with the values topic is that it offers no way out except to break off the relationship. Which seems like a pretty dramatic way to deal with a misplaced toilet seat. The amazing thing is, many human couples do just that. They use every disagreement to prove to the other their superiority, and that the only mistake they made was to marry the other person.

Arguments do not break up marriages. Happy couples disagree all the time. Topics, the wrong topics, break up marriages. Values—good and bad—make the worst topic for staying together.

Not that you shouldn't have values. A sense of right and wrong is a good thing. It's just that this makes for a lousy argument over a toilet seat. The values argument leads to anger.

To improve the mood in the room, you don't want to prosecute your partner. That's the blame topic. Nor do you want to show that the toilet seat proves him a terrible person. That's values. So are you doomed? Does your partner's thoughtlessness lead inevitably to a life alone with your cat?

No. Because there's a third topic. This one can save an argument, and even a marriage.

## *Topic: choice*

*"How are we going to keep this from happening again?"*

In the best arguments, you offer a choice or decision. You come up with a solution to a problem. Your spouse might disagree with your solution, but he proposes a choice of his own. That's what you argue about. You don't accuse each other. You don't use the toilet seat as proof of each other's criminality. Instead, you look at the problem and talk about how to solve it. You make a choice. Suddenly the topic is no longer about what the man did, or what kind of a husband he is, but about solving the problem together.

Easy for us to say, right? How can you think of choosing the best topic when you're furious at someone or getting yelled at yourself?

Here's a trick. Instead of thinking about the topic—blame, values or choice—go back to grammar lessons. Think about what *tense* you should be in: past, present or future.

Blame has to do with a crime committed in the *past*.
Values is all about the *present*: who's good and
    who's bad.

Choices deal with the *future*—a fix that makes for a
   better tomorrow and drier cats.

So here is the most useful tool to take the anger out of
a human argument: Switch to the future. If you're the victim, avoid focusing on the crime. Whatever you do, avoid
attributing the crime to some character flaw in the perpetrator. Instead, talk about what choice to make to keep
the thing from happening again. You chose the moment.
You chose the medium. Now you choose the future.

   You: I see you left the toilet seat up again. I went online
          and found a device that closes it automatically. We
          could spend the money, or you could get in the
          habit of closing the lid.

This approach does not ensure perfect behavior. The
blighter may promise to close the lid and then forget again.
Some highly intelligent spouses, especially the male ones,
suffer a serious mental block when it comes to toilet lids. (It
may have something to do with the kidneys. And maybe
the Y chromosome.) But at least the neighbors won't hear
you yelling at each other. The relationship stays intact. And
the bathroom may get a bit safer for thirsty cats.

## Cats can be futurists too

No self-respecting cat would leave the toilet seat up in the
first place. (But if someone has already left it up, he thanks

36

them.) But suppose the cat is angry with you for something you did—or failed to do. Suppose Natalie agreed to take care of a neighbor's kitten for a few hours, in her (and Charlie's) home. Charlie gets upset, understandably. This is a serious violation of his personal space.

Now, Charlie is a reasonable cat. (Some cats are not. Females in particular can be as territorial as male humans.) He is wise enough to know that he might get something out of this situation, like a treat.

> Natalie: Don't worry, Charlie. This adorable little kitten is only here for a while. You and I will be alone together in just a few hours.
> Charlie: [*Looks pathetic.*]
> Natalie: Aww, come on, Charlie. Here's a treat.

Excellent negotiation, Charlie! Honestly, some cats, and very few humans, are as sophisticated as this. If you want to salvage a bad situation, you have to think about the future. Otherwise you have nothing but anger. When you're facing an upset person, try switching the tense to the future. If that fails, remove the cause of their anger (scrawny cat, open toilet seat) and back off.

## *Living in the now makes some cats and all people tribal*

Gurus and New Age types tell us to be really present and to live in the now. There's a lot to this philosophy. It has produced many happy cats. But the present is a very tribal tense, especially when there's a disagreement. The present is all about values, and about who's good or bad, who's in or out of the clan. Cats think of Good People and Good Cats, just as they think about Good Things and Bad Things. Good People provide Good Things and smell familiar. Good Cats smell like family. A Good Person who does a bad thing, such as stepping on a cat's tail, may temporarily not qualify as a Good Person. But as long as you behave yourself, providing more Good Things, you'll soon be back in the cat's good graces.

Here's the thing: Cats, despite their reputation, do not bear grudges. They simply decide Right from Wrong. If you're permanently Wrong (a Bad Person), a cat still won't bear a grudge. She'll simply hate you.

# Dignity won't get your belly rubbed.

So you embarrassed yourself.
Be like a cat and leave the past behind.

# 4. Fit In with the Clan: The Box Maneuver

*Practice perfect decorum*

"Ignorant people think it is the noise which fighting cats make that is so aggravating, but it ain't so; it is the sickening grammar that they use."

—Mark Twain

People often think of persuasion as a kind of battle, even if it's a friendly battle. Word fact: "Debate" comes from the same Latin word as "battle." But every cat owner has been persuaded by a cat—and not one cat has ever persuaded through debate. Instead, the cat uses different tools. One of them is **decorum**. We think of decorum as "proper" grammar. Or good manners, such as holding your pinky out when you use the can opener. The thing is, what is good manners for one group may be terrible manners for another. Throw a pool party for dogs and they will declare you Saint Bernard. Throw a pool party for cats and—well, that's just rude. For many cats, it is polite to put them up on your shoulders. For most dogs, not so polite. The same goes for people. Slapping a teammate on the butt after a goal might be perfectly acceptable, while slapping a business partner on the butt . . . not so.

But are we talking just about manners here? No.

Decorum is more than the rules that make you seem polite. It also has to do with whether your audience finds you agreeable. In fact, "decorum" comes from the Latin word for "fitness." As in, "fitting in." Every animal and human thrives when it fits perfectly in its environment. Decorum means fitting into a social environment.

It's true that decorum depends on politeness. But politeness means being considerate. It means taking into account other people's attitudes and feelings. Some cultures consider it good manners to eat with your hands. If you are invited to dinner with these people, should you insist on a fork and knife? Or, worse, insist that everybody else use a fork and knife? Not if you want to practice decorum.

## Grammar ain't for all y'all

Besides fitting into the manners of other people, decorum means fitting into people's language as well. It's important to learn grammar in school, not because "good grammar" necessarily makes more sense than "bad" or is somehow morally superior, but because learning so-called proper grammar lets you communicate with the elite. Grammar enables a kid who grew up in poverty to speak with kings and CEOs. On the other hand, how should a grandmother who hates rap music speak to young lovers of that music?

> Grandmother: What if one is conversing with young people for whom proper grammar seems almost a foreign language?

That very question might mystify some young people. They may have trouble understanding her. At the very least, this perfectly grammatical sentence would not help Grandma fit in at a rap record label.

Fussy, formal grammar can turn off even highly educated people. Winston Churchill once called rules-bound speech—the kind that goes to any length to avoid putting a preposition at the end of a sentence—"errant pedantry up with which I will not put."

So how does a grandmother hold a conversation with kids who speak like the lyrics of the songs on their playlists? If she wants to complain about the males in her family leaving toilet lids up, does she say, "Boys be like leavin' lids up alla time?"

Not unless she usually talks like that. (Some grandmothers definitely do talk like that.)

But don't take our word for it. Ask a cat.

Literally. Let's have Natalie, who definitely is not a grandmother, ask her cat.

> Natalie: Charlie, how should I speak to young people who like to pretend they're hip-hop artists?

Wait for the answer. Chances are, Charlie will wisely say nothing. He will give Natalie a polite look (Charlie is a very decorous cat) and walk away. Or, if he does say something, the sentence will not be highly grammatical. But it will be perfectly correct for a cat.

The same thing goes with grammar. If you are talking to someone who loves "proper" grammar, the kind taught

43

in grammar class, then speaking her kind of language makes you fit in.

Proper decorum is tricky. You want to avoid appearing to try too hard. For example, a human should never meow at a cat. An animal of a different species expects you to speak like a human. Instead, you want to act the way a good human would act with a cat. Instead of meowing, sit still and let the cat come to you. Cats know that a good sniff at your shoe will tell them volumes. Similarly, a grandmother trying to communicate with teenagers should speak the way teenagers would want a good grand-mother to speak—not as a snob, but respectfully. And a teenager should do the same with a well-educated grand-mother. How would Grandma expect a good teenager to speak?

## *Unstiff thy neck*

Tactfulness is another kind of decorum. Hurting people's feelings, even when you're telling the blunt truth, pushes them away from you.

None of which really means being yourself. This decorum might even be kind of manipulative. You may prefer the attitude, "This is me. Take it or leave it."

(Admittedly, some cats have this attitude as well. Not every cat is perfect.)

But adapting to your social environment does not have to mean betraying your true self. Just make sure your true self is not a total stiff-neck.

That's in the Book of Exodus.

God tells Moses that he has taken a gander at Moses's people and is not impressed. "Behold," God says. "They are a stiff-necked people." That means they are unchanging, unadaptable. Don't be so holier-than-thou "true" to yourself to the point where you fail to adapt to your social environment. You're just a stiff-neck.

A great cure for a stiff neck is to pay close attention to the group you're with, and to convince yourself that the group pleases you.

(Another good cure: A neck scratch, working back from behind the ears. Oh, that feels good.)

But wait. What does all this have to do with persuasion and cats?

Remember, persuasion starts with agreeability. To get an agreement, at least one of you has to be agreeable. If your person or cat finds you the right sort, that you fit in, then you're much more likely to get what you want. If your audience thinks you have a stiff neck, then they are more likely to hiss at you or run away and hide.

To fit in, a cat does not have to pretend to be a human. He simply has to show how much he enjoys humans. The same goes for you. Instead of trying to speak like a teenager, a grown-up has only to seem to enjoy teenagers.

As a cat will show you, this kind of decorum is a lot like purring.

## *The art of the purr*

A purr is a two-way rhetorical statement. It says, "I'm happy to be with you." And it also says, "Whatever you're doing, please do more."

A purr acts like a kind of drug on us humans, putting us in a docile, manageable state. Cats use the purr to control us. It works.

The good news is we can do almost as well as a cat, creating effects that work like a purr.

First, you should act as though you love to be with your audience. This is true whether you're petting a cat or speaking to a group of humans. Every cat knows that the "happy to be with you" part of a purr is crucial to getting the extra petting. In rhetoric this is called **ingratiation**. It means putting yourself in someone's good graces. We like to call it "agreeability." By making yourself agreeable, you make the other person more likely to agree with you. It's like a purr without the rumble-in-the-chest part.

Whenever you want something from someone, think to yourself, "I'm happy to be with you." Think this even if it is not exactly true—even if the other people are unpleasant. The interesting thing is, pretending to like people can actually make them more bearable.

One reason your cat purrs:
It makes *you* more bearable to the cat.

Even people have been known to purr. For example, people who meditate often say the word "om" deep down,

46

getting those vibrations to massage their innards. People enjoying a restaurant's So Sinful You're Going Straight to Hell Chocolate Cake often purr while forking the stuff into their mouths. After all, what is "mmmm" but a messy purr? And what about when we moan during a back rub or, you know, other activities?

Right. Purring.

In a conversation with a cat or a human, try purring *rhetorically*. Put yourself in a pleasing, ingratiating mood. (Skip the rumble, which can be creepy when you're just talking. Leave the actual conversational purr to the feline experts.) By changing your mood, you can improve the mood of others. Show pleasure in the relationship before you try to talk people into things.

Purr first, then steer.

Scientists confirm what cats have known all along: To put someone in the mood to be persuaded, make him feel happy, comfortable and in control of the situation.

A teenager finds herself in dire need of her mother's car. Before she barges up and says, "May I borrow the car?", she should start her mental purr. Remembering all the nice things Mom has done for her. Thinking of all the sacrifices Mom made. Thinking what a basically good person Mom is, even if she often fails to recognize that her daughter is not a kid anymore. Just thinking the best of her, in a purring way. This works much better than sucking up to Mom or complimenting her looks. (Mothers see right through flattery.)

Moods tend to be infectious. A purring cat causes another cat to purr. Same thing with mothers. The daughter may not actually get the car. (Stay tuned for other tools.) But at least they both will have a nice moment, which in the long run will help the girl get what she wants. This is something most cats know better than humans: A strong relationship wins more treats. Bearing grudges won't even earn a decent lap.

Another purring trick: Pretend to be satisfied even when you're *not* getting exactly what you want. A cat will purr even when her idiot "master" scratches the wrong part. The cat wants a chin rub, and the fool keeps scratching away at her back. What does the cat do? She purrs, and purrs some more, and then lifts her head meaningfully.

We have a lot to learn from cats.

## *Make yourself comfortable*

Cats can be mistaken for practicing bad decorum. For example, one who insists on jumping on to the dinner table might not seem all that polite. But perhaps he sees things otherwise. After all, *you* are eating at the dinner table. And it is rather rude that you have not provided him with a high-enough chair. But he is not one to bear grudges. He is perfectly happy to sit on the table to share your turkey.

In other words, it can be hard for one species to understand another animal's rules for behavior. And, you have to admit, human rules are pretty strange.

To see how excellent cats can be at the art of fitting in,

just look at what happens when you open a small package from Amazon and put the box on the floor. How do cats manage to squeeze into such a tiny cardboard space? And how do they get up on high shelves and hide behind a thicket of paperback books?

They crawl, squeeze and insinuate like magic. How do they do that? They *adapt*. They shape their bodies to fit the spaces.

We humans fail to think this way often enough. We like to shape our surroundings to us instead of the other way around. This makes us very good architects and terrible campers. Still, thinking more like a cat than a human can actually make us better at decorum with other humans.

Imagine a social setting as a small, intimate space. You want to fit into that space. It would be a mistake to treat other people the way we treat our environment, shaping it to fit us rather than adapting ourselves to it.

How often do you make that mistake, gathering friends who agree with you most of the time? We live in communities where people look like us and think the same way. We even tend to hire people who seem like us. Most of the time, this approach makes us comfortable.

But now and then we find ourselves in an awkward place, such as an office party or a town meeting or a job interview. We have no choice but to try to fit in. The only thing we can do is adapt.

You're a guest at a party, and a man who has had one too many wine coolers tries to pick a political fight with you. When he fails to get a rise out of you, he yells that you support "the terrorists." You might feel the temptation to argue with him or make a cutting remark about wine-cooler abuse. But remember: You're in a social environment, one that contains more guests than just that drunk man. Think about decorum. In any conflict where there's an audience, the most decorous, fitting-in strategy means winning over the audience, not your attacker. Be like a cat: show dignity. Act like the better character. The other party guests will see you as one of them, and they'll love you for it. Congratulations! You fit your immediate surroundings.

The wise cat examines the box first, then adjusts his body to fit the box. This is not dishonesty. It's adaptability. Decorum is exactly the same thing: adaptability.

The adaptable life is an agreeable life.

# Use your kitty litter.

Good decorum means being discreet. Don't show your messes. And definitely don't show the messes your friends and littermates made.

# 5. Earn Loyalty:
# The Virtuous Scratch

*Wield the tools of character*

"When a cat flatters . . . he is not insincere:
you may safely take it for real kindness."
—Walter Savage Landor

At this point you may be wondering: When will we get to the persuasion part? What about the killer logic? The deadly phrase? The witty line that stops your opponent in his tracks?

We'll get to logic and wit later in the book. But ask yourself: Have you ever had a logical argument with a cat? Has a cat ever laughed at your fine wit?

Thought not.

Those skills do come in handy, especially if you argue with a human now and then. We'll even show you how to use logic with a cat. But the most important tools of persuasion have to do with whether your opponent thinks you're worth rubbing up to. You want him to think you're agreeable. That you fit in with the herd. You want him to feel less angry by thinking about the future.

And, most of all, you want him to like and trust you. That's what this chapter is about.

Both cats and humans prefer listening to people they think have a good character. We're sure you are a perfectly nice person. (You love cats, don't you? That right there makes you a nice person.) But being good is not enough. You have to make strangers and angry cats think of you as a good egg. This takes some persuasion.

The good news is once your audience likes and trusts you, not only will they listen to you, they will often do what you want. Even, sometimes, if your audience is a cat.

So let's look at how to polish your character. Call it your image if you like. The ancient Greeks called it **ethos**. It means "character," as other people and cats see it. A great ethos makes a great leader. Someone so well liked and trusted that all sorts and species want to follow her.

To earn a first-class ethos, you need to work on three traits of leadership: **caring**, **craft** and **cause**.

## *Always provide a lap*

Caring has to do with making your audience believe you put its interests ahead of your own. You want only what's best for them, even if that means giving up your favorite chair, or sacrificing a sweater to make the perfect curl-up blanket.

This is often harder to do with people. Cats almost always let you know what's in their best interest. People, not so much. You can feed a spouse at the same time every day, and that still might not earn her loyalty. She may really want a vacation. Or praise for getting a promotion at work. Or your awareness that her hair looks different.

That's why the first job of caring, ethos-wise, is to discover your audience's interest. What do they want? Doctors sometimes make the mistake of thinking it's enough to write a prescription. Most patients also want attention. (So do most cats.) When an uncaring doctor makes a mistake, he is much more likely to get sued. Patients will cut a caring doctor more slack. And what's a caring doctor? One who spends more time with the patient than he's required to, or who understands why it's so hard to stay on a diet.

The same idea applies to us non-doctors. If our co-workers think we're willing to sacrifice our time and effort for them, they will cover for us when we screw up. Ditto for our bosses, not to mention politicians and other leaders. Think Gandhi and Martin Luther King. Think Mother Teresa. The first two caused revolutions. The third became a saint. People wanted to follow these leaders, who cared about them. All three understood what was in the best interest of their audiences. That is how they got to be so loved.

How do you get a human to think you're caring? The obvious way is actually to care. Find out what your audience needs, and do your best day after day to meet those needs.

But that's not persuasion, which works faster. To persuade someone that you're a caring person, you need to do two things. First, show you understand. Second, offer to make some little sacrifice.

Boyfriend: I'm totally stressed out about the math exam.

Caring girlfriend: Why don't I skip the bonfire party and
    help you study?

Be careful. Sympathy does more for your ethos than just
fixing the problem. And definitely don't just give advice.

Girlfriend: My back is killing me from stacking those
    shelves.
Boyfriend: You need to go to the gym more. Get those
    back muscles in shape. And maybe lose a few pounds
    while you're at it.

This does not help your ethos. Instead, look sad and
offer a massage.

A cat does not need such complicated psychology. To
get your cat to think you have a caring ethos, just stay at
home. Never go on a business trip or a vacation. Drop
whatever you're doing whenever a lap is needed. Get off
the phone with your boss and open a can of tuna.

See what we're doing here? We show that we understand what's in the cat's best interest. And we let the cat
know we're willing to do whatever it takes to meet those
interests.

This does not mean giving in to every request. A cat is
smart enough to know that some unpleasant things are in
his best interest. Suppose he's a knucklehead who swallows
ribbons. He won't resent you if you pull a ribbon out of
his gullet now and then. And he will probably understand
if you keep the ribbons in a locked drawer.

It may sound hard to convince a cat that you care only

for her. But a true cat lover knows that it's much easier to convince a cat of your love than a human. A cat simply assumes there's no one else in your life. A human will always wonder.

## *The exact right place to scratch*

Craft means making an audience believe you're really good at the important stuff. You know what to do on every occasion. The ancients called this trait "practical wisdom." That's because craft is more than book learning. It takes practical experience for a teacher to know just when his students are getting bored, and to know what to do to get their attention back. A medical student can get an A in anatomy class and still not be ready to perform an appendectomy. Craft—practical wisdom—takes study plus experience.

With humans, you can give the impression of craft without teaching a class or taking out an appendix. One way is to use jargon—the right jargon. If you don't know the special words that a group uses, don't talk too much. Listen for those words and the way the group uses them. You can hurt the craft part of your ethos by using the wrong words. Older people make younger people laugh when they say they'll "Twitter" the news. (Far better to learn what Snapchat is.) If you want to impress someone with your car knowledge, know the difference between a lug wrench and a socket wrench. And know which one can help replace the shocks.

Cats are not so much concerned about words. To a cat, of course, the most important thing of all is to serve the cat. A person who does good craft knows exactly the right place to scratch a particular cat. That person also provides food exactly on time, and sometimes early. The right toys get bought. The beds are comfortable and never in a cold place.

Want a person to trust you? Use the right words to send a group email. Want a cat to trust you? Deal with that over-friendly dog, the one with no cat manners.

Either way, you show you know what you're doing. That's craft.

## The smell test

Cause has to do with your ability to represent a Good Thing. You stand for something larger than the usual day-to-day concerns. Corporations often try to convince us that they represent good causes and don't just grub after profits. Banks talk about giving customers "freedom." Fast-food joints fight for your right to have anything you want on your hamburger. Fancy cars and watches represent quality in an ugly, underdesigned world. And many of us fall for that stuff, spending more money than we should, because we believe we're giving money to a Good Thing. And that makes us feel good ourselves.

In rhetoric, cause is called **virtue**. These days we think virtue describes an old-fashioned kind of girl. (Does anybody even talk about virtue anymore?) But in the really old days—the old days of a thousand and more years ago—virtue was something men were supposed to have even more than women. It meant standing for something bigger than themselves. While caring is about the interest of your audience, cause is about a higher interest. Such as God, country, the environment or rescuing stray cats.

In other words, cause is about values. Not your values, necessarily. The audience's values. Suppose your audience thinks that jobs are more important than the environment. You will not help your ethos by talking about saving the whales. Far better to talk about providing jobs for everybody.

Does that mean you should be a chameleon? Pretend you stand for things you don't care about? Or, worse, go against your own beliefs?

No. But it does mean understanding what your audience values. And it means honoring those values. If what your audience values is evil, then maybe you shouldn't be talking to those people in the first place. But if you simply don't share those same values, then you can still honor them. They're good people, doing the best they can.

Some people think football is a bad sport. Kids get hurt and the music is terrible. Other people think football is what made America great. You can hate football and still honor football fans for loving football. That's rhetoric at its best. You don't have to pretend to like football. If you honor the fans, they will think you are a virtuous person.

But you still need to make that audience believe you stand for something. Just make sure you stand for values that you both share. So you don't like football. Maybe you love nachos. Or cheerleaders. Or maybe you tear up at the national anthem. That's a cause a lot of audiences can believe in. Your ethos is getting better already.

Cats are harder to convince this way. They can see right through a cause, unless it has to do with Good Things like food and laps. That's partly because cats think about good and bad people more simply than the rest of us. If you smell like family, you're family. And smelling like family means hanging around a lot, because that's what family does. Humans develop loyalties to one another based on what movies they like and how they feel about immigration and taxes, but that doesn't really do much to separate the Good from the Bad.

Maybe we need to develop more of a cat's sense of smell.

Caring, craft and cause are the three traits that cats and people use to judge character. The difference is that you can fake these things with humans. Human rhetoric is all about the impression you make, whether it's true or not. Now, it is easier to give a good impression if you really are a good person. But think of all those politicians who get themselves elected, all those false prophets and gangsters and super-salespeople with dark hearts who make people love them. Abraham Lincoln said that you can't fool all of the people all of the time. He was setting a pretty low bar for humanity. While you can fool all of the people some of the time, and some of the people all of the time, you cannot fool a single cat for very long. If you are not a good

Cat Person, he will see right through you. He will know you're not a Good Person. So the best way to gain the love and respect of a cat is to practice genuine caring, craft and cause. Devote yourself to a cat. Be excellent at play and mealtimes. And, mostly, be there. When it comes to cats, that's your cause.

People, being people, need to practice more of the rhetorical arts to gain respect. Suppose you're a genuinely good person, good at what you do, and you get far too little appreciation for it. You need to monitor how well you project your concern for others, your ability to solve problems on the fly and your fight for a greater good. Check your résumé and see if it projects all three traits. When you do a good thing, don't just do it in front of the mirror. Let people see your wonderfulness. It will do wonders for your reputation among humans.

But not among cats.

CAT WISDOM

# Virtue lies in steady habits.

Sleep, eat and do everything else regularly, at the exact same time each day. Habits are what make cats so virtuous.

# 6. Argue Logically: The Deductive Mousetrap

*Get a cat to come*

"When Rome burned, the emperor's cats still
expected to be fed on time."
—Seanan McGuire

Of course you can never *make* a cat come. It comes when it wants to. Dog lovers often point this out. They think cats are self-centered and egotistical. This attitude gets cats all wrong. Being reasonable creatures, cats need a reason. They come when it's an obviously good idea.

One excellent reason is food. Call a cat during mealtime and she will trot right over. She may run to the kitchen even when you call her before mealtime.

See? Told you cats come. Just not always the way you wish they would.

A comfortable scratch is another reason to come. Most cats like to be scratched and, having an excellent vocabulary, will come when you offer a scratch.

A favorite toy: also a good reason.
Catnip: duh.
Lap: also obvious.

Now, if you fail to come up with a good reason, a cat will reasonably ask, "Why should I?" To a dog lover, this question may sound rude. Dogs are creatures of the mine-is-not-to-reason-why point of view. But if you listen closely to a cat during the day, you will realize that *he* often asks *you* to come. Yet how often do you obey? A wise cat—and most cats are very wise—will not resent you when you fail to do so. He understands that he needs to offer a better reason. So he changes his tone, calling more loudly and insistently until the reason to come is to stop the yowling. Or he looks at you with giant Bambi eyes and just opens his mouth. Most humans obey the Silent Meow instantly. They're kind of stupid that way.

Humans don't always come when a human calls, either.

Boyfriend: Come over.
Girlfriend: Now?
Boyfriend: Yeah.
Girlfriend: Why?
Boyfriend: Do you need a reason?
Girlfriend: Yeah.

This is where persuasion comes in—not only to get a person or a cat to come but to get them to do what you want in general. A reason does not have to be a bribe. Or even a fact.

## *The logical jab and cross*

Okay, now we have to use a term that may be unfamiliar to you. Unlike cats, many humans tend to shy away from strange words. The most important building block in persuasive logic is—wait for it—the **enthymeme** (EN-the-meem). It's a great word to pronounce if you want to intimidate someone; a human, I mean. Big words don't intimidate cats.

An enthymeme is a one-two logical punch, like boxing's jab and cross. You just need two pieces:

1. The proof. Call it "the reason," if you like.
2. The conclusion.

Proof: I smell tuna salad on the kitchen counter.
Conclusion: I should jump up onto the counter.

As you can see, cats are very good at enthymemes. Humans, not so much.

First human: I don't want to go to the Renaissance Fair.
Second human: Why not?
First human: I just don't, that's why not.

This is not an enthymeme. In an enthymeme, every conclusion needs a reason. A reason can't be the conclusion itself. "I don't want to go because I don't want to go" chases its own tail, like a dog.

Let's try again.

First human: I don't want to go to the Renaissance Fair.
Second human: Why not?
First human: I heard there will be Morris dancers.

Excellent enthymeme. The proof—the threat of bands of annoying dancers with bells and sticks—supports the conclusion that the Renaissance Fair is a bad idea. As you can see, either part of the enthymeme can go first, the proof or the conclusion.

I heard there will be Morris dancers, so I don't want to go.
   I don't want to go, because there may be Morris dancers.

Cats know this already.

Bootlaces are fun. Therefore, they're a toy.
   Bootlaces are toys, because they're fun. Especially when a human is trying to tie them.

You just can't beat excellent logic like that. If you ever get confused about what an enthymeme does, just think of why a cat comes. It reaches a conclusion to come if you give her a good reason. In persuasion, a conclusion usually involves a choice ("I think I'll come") or an action (coming).

Got it? Then you're ahead of most people. Including politicians. And speaking of politicians, the enthymeme is the single best way to tell if someone is talking nonsense or trying to manipulate you.

Let's see how by looking more closely at reasons—the

"proof" part of an enthymeme. It's a great way of spotting BS and—if you're the devious type—manipulating other people.

## *A fact is what your audience thinks is a fact*

A reason often starts with a fact.

The sun comes up at the same time this morning as it did yesterday morning. Therefore, the cat knows you should get up exactly at that time, despite what the clock says. The sunrise is a fact.

One plus one equals two: Another fact. Add one new cat to a single-cat household and you get a pair of spitting cats. As a human, you know that one cat plus one cat equals two cats.

But even a solid fact can get a different spin, depending on the audience. If you're not a morning person and lack a cat, the sunrise may be just a theory. To your original cat, one cat plus one cat equals one cat too many.

Every fact can get a different interpretation. One audience may think that tuna-flavored stool softener makes a delicious dessert. Another may find this disgusting.

When it comes to persuasion, what your audience believes can be more important than the facts themselves. If your audience doesn't believe that liver paste is good for it, then that fact will fail to persuade it. Your audience may believe that eating a turkey that outweighs it is a good idea. The fact that eating the turkey will make your audience sick won't be convincing.

Naturally, we're talking about humans.

People wish that arguments were all about facts and logic. But useful arguments have to do with choices, such as whether or not to come. A choice is not a fact. And the main elements affecting a choice usually have to do with what the audience believes or expects. If the audience believes that coming will end up in a good meal or a luxurious scratch, then it will be persuaded.

Therefore not all proofs or reasons have to start with facts. If a cat or a human believes something to be true, she will be persuaded just as if that belief were a real fact. If a person believes that a house is haunted, she will refuse to buy the house—whether ghosts exist or not.

A cat will chase an alluring red laser dot in the perfect belief that the dot is a fast-moving glowing bug. A bug that a human controls with a small stick. Perfectly reasonable—more reasonable than a belief in ghosts—if not exactly true. So if you can get a cat or a human to believe something, or if you start with something they already believe, then you can use that belief as if it's a fact.

A moving red dot is a bug. Therefore it should be hunted.

Beliefs come from two sources: *experience* and *expectation*. Your average cat has had extensive and enjoyable experiences with bugs. He expects anything that acts like a bug to be equally fun.

On the opposite end of the fun spectrum, a cat who jumps onto a hot woodstove will have a bad experience. From now on, he will steer a wide berth around hot woodstoves. But, as Mark Twain observed, he will also avoid jumping on cold woodstoves. That's because he expects every woodstove to be hot. His previous experience tells him that woodstoves are hot. This leads to the expectation that future woodstoves will be equally hot. And so he believes that woodstoves make very bad places to jump on to. Better safe than sorry.

Cats can form a strong belief with just one experience. They're quick learners. Give a cat a new treat, and if she likes it, she will expect that treat for the rest of her life. The experience leads to expectation, which leads to the belief that the treat is a Good Thing. Cats are wise enough to understand that no Good Thing should come to an end.

People are much slower learners. They often need two or three disasters to get them to believe anything. Elected officials are even worse; they require decades of disasters.

If you want to persuade someone, it's fine to marshal good facts. But the persuasion part comes when you speak to what your audience believes. Suppose you're a manager of an office and the people higher up in the company have asked you to increase productivity. You could gather everyone together and project slides showing how much more productive the other divisions are. Or you could put up cool-looking graphs that perfectly illustrate how much more work would get done if everyone came to work half an hour earlier. Would the slides persuade your colleagues to put in the extra time or effort? Not in any office we've worked in.

Instead, you want to listen first. Try to pick up what people in the office already believe. You hear that they feel overworked and underappreciated. They feel powerless.

So, instead of relying exclusively on facts and statistics, you work from your coworkers' beliefs:

> You: We've been given a challenge by the C suite. How are we going to increase productivity? I'm going to need your best ideas. Let's come back in a week. Tell me what we can be doing better. And if we succeed, I'll make sure the C suite hears about it, and I'll fight for rewarding your effort.

Now, maybe your office mates are not so overworked, and you happen to have been a great listener all along. In rhetoric, these truths do not matter. People know what they believe, just as cats know what they believe. And while their beliefs may be wrong, for persuasion purposes, they're perfectly logical.

Cats can be just as stupid as humans when it comes to facts. Anyone who has ever used a laser pointer with a cat knows that his grip on reality can be a little shaky. Cats are also very good at ignoring facts that don't agree with them.

> You: No, I'm not going to give you another treat. You're getting fat.
> Cat: [*Meaningful silence.*]

## *Habits make things real*

A cat can turn a Good Thing into a habit, so long as the human cooperates. And a habit is as good as the truth.

This may be hard for a human to understand, so it's worth repeating: *A habit is as good as the truth.*

This is not as complicated as it sounds. The sun comes up every day. From the sun's point of view, that's a habit. Based on our experience of every other sunrise, we can expect the sun to come up tomorrow, and the next day, and the next. Our experience leads to that expectation. That's belief. (It's also a fallacy, called the **fallacy of antecedent**. While the sun seems fairly reliable so long as we avoid blowing up the Earth, it's a fallacy to believe that you should drive fast because you've never had an accident.) When you or an audience or a cat believe something to be true, from the standpoint of persuasion, it's as good as the truth. So, in the art of rhetoric, the sun's habit of getting up every morning is a true thing.

As you know, cats are very good at habits, and as predators they are experts at observing the habits of other species, including mice, birds and humans. "You can observe a lot by just watching," said Yogi Berra. (He was a cat in a past life.) And the habits of others become truths. If you rise at the same time every morning, your alarm is as true as the sun, from the cat's point of view.

On the other hand, not getting up at the regular time is a kind of lie to a cat. That's why the switch from daylight-saving to standard time, when we get up an hour later, can upset a sensitive cat.

Which is another piece of wisdom we should take from cats. Steady habits are a set of truths. They make up who we are. Straying from a good habit, practiced long enough, should seem like a lie. That's because a belief comes from experience and expectation. In cats, experience and expectation are the same thing. This is very wise.

If you ever want to persuade yourself to eat properly, think like a cat. Don't try to motivate yourself. Instead, try to gain a habit. If you tend to skip breakfast only to wolf down a Danish midmorning, make yourself a smoothie. Pack it with things you don't like and probably would not eat when fully awake, like spinach and chia seeds and unflavoured yogurt. Force it down every day until it becomes a habit. If you ever skip that smoothie in the future, it will seem somehow morally wrong. Now you know how a cat thinks.

What's a habit but a long, serial experience?

A habit builds the expectation that you'll do the same thing over again. And an expectation, in the world of persuasion, is the same as the truth.

Of course, a cat is happy to let you give her an unexpected treat. Steady habits are good, but you should not get neurotic about them. In fact, go ahead and turn that sudden treat into a regular habit. She won't mind at all.

What does all this have to do with getting a cat to come when you call? Everything. In order for the cat to come, she has to believe that coming is a Good Thing, a kind of truth. If coming isn't a Good Thing, then it isn't true, for cats know that all Good Things are true. And by Good Things, I mean from the cat's point of view, not yours.

# Never eat a ladybug.

When dazzled by beauty or eloquence, remember:
If it's as cute as a bug, it probably tastes like one.

# 7. Avoid Manipulation: The Magical Bookshelf

*Logical fallacies, and why they fool us*

> "Anyone who believes what a cat tells him deserves all he gets."
>
> —Neil Gaiman

Up until now we have covered the delightful ways to persuade cats and people. But one of the most important reasons to learn these tools is to keep from being persuaded ourselves. Unless we *want* to be persuaded.

We cat owners often love it when a cat manipulates us. It puts things on an even footing, species-wise. Besides, what's the fun in having an ingenuous cat? You might as well have a dog.

It is much less fun to be seduced by a fellow human, unless that human is a lover. Salespeople, marketers and politicians use tricks that get us to buy things we don't want. Or to spend money we don't have. Or to live in terror of things that shouldn't scare us. Or even to hate perfectly nice people and age-old religions.

Persuasion is a dark art. If you want to make it less dark, shine a light on it. To stop those manipulators from having their way with you, you can learn two of their most powerful tools: **facade words** and **fallacies**. Both of them have to do with the logical part of rhetoric. Or, rather, the illogical part.

The first tool messes with the definitions of words.

## *A toy is a toy is a toy*

One of the surest signs that a person lacks a clue is when he says, "Something's going on." You hear people say this in politics all the time. "Something's going on." You also hear politicians talk about war when they don't really mean war. The war against the middle class. The war against white people.

And then there's "they." They are ruining our country. They are invading.

You know what these words are? They're facades. Like the walls of the saloons and stores on a Western movie set, these words can look real. But look behind them and there's nothing there. No meaning at all.

The most powerful vaccine against facade words is a simple phrase: *What do you mean by . . . ?*

When you hear someone say, "Something's going on," ask, "What do you mean by 'something'?" And for that matter, "What do you mean by 'going on'?" Has the something been going on for a while? Is the something increasing? What problems is that something causing?

Same with "war." A war is a serious thing. Many people

die in them. Whole cities, even civilizations, can get destroyed. Sure, the middle class may be hurting. Another class may be hurting the middle class—or it might be corporations or trade agreements or whatever you believe—but have there been drone strikes? Boots on the ground? Prisoners taken?

And anytime someone talks about a group of people as "they" without being very specific, ask the question: "Who do you mean by 'they'?"

The question serves as a cannonball knocking down the fake saloon front. Once you've done that, take a look at what the facade is made of.

The "war" word is a metaphor. It plays pretend. Look at a field of grain and call it an ocean: You're pretending that the rippling stalks are waves. No harm in that. Nobody is going to try to float a boat on top of that wheat. But metaphors get nasty when people take them too literally. When someone defending the middle class against "war" starts talking about "the enemy," you're in dangerous territory.

Cats are much more sensible than we are about playing pretend. A cat toy is pretend prey. True, your cat might get carried away and try to eat it. But pretty soon she will come to her senses.

A metaphor, in turn, is a kind of **trope**. Tropes are words that play pretend. One of the sneakiest tropes is one most of us haven't heard of. It's called the **synecdoche** (sin-ECK-doe-kee). A synecdoche takes a part of a group and pretends it's the whole group. One immigrant

79

commits a crime, and your nastier politician will pretend that immigrants are criminals. In the olden days, rich people all looked like one particular fat, cigar-smoking millionaire named Andrew Carnegie. People started calling him a "fat cat." In some circles that might be a compliment. But the term probably hurt some rich people's feelings. And many cats.

Tropes are tricky things, even if you know how to pronounce them. But *pronouns* can be just as sneaky. The word "they" is a pronoun. This is where grammar can come in handy. A pronoun's home base is the word it stands for. That home word is the **antecedent**. When somebody uses a pronoun—"it," "they," "them"—search for the antecedent. Think whether a home word came before it—say, "immigration," "immigrants." Then think about those immigrants and whether the speaker is making any sense about them.

Our brains like to make connections between things. We see a few colors and assume a flag. We hear a few notes and can sing the rest of the song. This ability makes us brilliant. We can see a few rocks and imagine building a castle. It's why humans rule the world instead of cats. But that same trait can make us leap to wrong conclusions. We see a kind of tattoo and assume a gang member. Or we hear an accent and assume a terrorist. Politicians play off this conclusion-leaping. They use our leaping to manipulate us.

Not so with cats. Being predators, they think more simply. If they fail to understand us, it's probably our fault.

Man speaking to his lover: You're toying with my
feelings.

The cat hears "toy" and comes running. To a cat, a toy
is a toy and not a trope.

If all this makes you feel like a confused cat, try this
remedy. If "What do you mean by . . . ?" fails to clear
things up, ask for details:

Who exactly?
How many?
When?

Who are these "they?" How many of them are there?
Are their numbers growing? When did they get here?

If that doesn't work, then ask for sources.

You: Where'd you hear that?

Think about those sources. Is it your great-aunt
who just joined Facebook? Or a peer-reviewed science
journal?

Remember to ask for these three things:

1. Definitions.
2. Details.
3. Sources.

The other person might find your questions annoying.
But they can actually help him talk sense. Being forced to
think about facts, definitions and details can actually make
a crazy-sounding person talk less crazy.

Opponent: Okay, maybe not all immigrants. Maybe not
   even most of them.

Tropes and pronouns fool people more than cats. Know
what fools both species? Fallacies.

## *The mistaken hiss*

A fallacy is an argument that messes with logic.

One fallacy gets committed when a cat makes an unrea-
sonable assumption about another cat. A female cat, for
instance, often dislikes other females. It's a territorial
thing. But a female cat won't just resent other female cats;
she will hiss and swipe at female humans as well.

Humans do exactly the same thing. They see a fictional
dark-skinned man commit a crime on television, and that
makes them scared of every real dark-skinned man. A little
kid throws a temper tantrum in a restaurant, and onlook-
ers think, *Kids these days . . .*

The fallacy is the same for both cats and humans. It's
called **hasty generalization**, making assumptions based
on just one or two examples or characteristics.

Why hasty? Because some carefully considered gener-
alizations often turn out to be true, at least most of the
time. For example, men are very bad at getting preg-
nant. This generalization seems to be true all the time. It's
colder in the winter than in the summer: true most of the
time. Women have higher voices than men: true much of
the time.

Anything measured with statistics is a generalization. If four out of five doctors like a particular brand of toothpaste, it's reasonable to think that doctors tend to like that toothpaste. But the tricky—and sometimes evil—side of hasty generalization comes when you're dealing with an individual. Statistically, women have weaker arms than men do. But that does not mean you're guaranteed to win an arm-wrestling contest with every woman. Boys tend to like trucks more than girls do. Does that mean a girl who likes trucks isn't really a girl? Even a cat wouldn't make that mistake. A cat would totally know that a girl with a truck is still a girl.

On the other hand, if you feed a cat at four in the morning, the cat will probably assume that breakfast should always happen at four in the morning. Cats are especially good at fallacies they like.

## A coincidence is not magic

Another fun, and dangerous, fallacy is the notion that when two things happen at the same time that means one thing *caused* the other. One particular cat (his name has been withheld upon request) thinks that sitting on a particular bookshelf will make dinnertime happen sooner. That's because he happened to jump on that shelf one time just when his human was getting ready for a date and served dinner early. *Hmmm,* the cat thought. *I jump on the bookshelf and dinner comes. Therefore, jumping on the bookshelf makes dinner come.* And so he set himself up for weeks of disappointment until he finally gave up the notion. (He continued to jump up on the bookshelf an hour before dinner, only now it was just a habit.)

Many human superstitions start with this same fallacy. A baseball player wears uncomfortable underwear while hitting a grand slam. From then on, that same tight, hole-pocked pair of underpants becomes part of his uniform. This fallacy has a fancy name: it's a **post hoc fallacy**, from the Latin *post hoc ergo propter hoc*, which means "after this, therefore because of this." People and cats commit this fallacy when they think that a correlation—one thing happening with something else—is a cause. Some parents resist getting life-saving vaccinations for their two-year-olds because some kids get diagnosed with autism soon after they get their shots. Autism is detectable just about the same age that kids get their two-year vaccinations. This leads a few parents to think that vaccinations cause autism, even though science has clearly proven they don't.

The post hoc fallacy tends to hit us in subtle ways. A student parties all night and aces an exam. Conclusion: Partying strengthens his mental faculties! Never mind that he was paying extra attention in class and had already read the material thoroughly.

Or you go on holiday and it rains the entire week. "I'm sorry," you say to the hotel manager. "I made it rain." Even if you were slightly kidding, you were committing an easy fallacy. If, however, you really did make it rain, you should switch careers. Farmers would pay you good money.

## *Close your eyes to make it go away*

If you have seen a cat hide by putting her head in a box with her butt sticking out, you have witnessed a fallacy doctors often commit. It goes like this: "If I can't see it, it doesn't exist." A cat will ignore something it doesn't like, with the healthy attitude that pretending it doesn't exist will make it more likely not to exist.

When a doctor does that same thing, it isn't so healthy. He tells you that the tests were negative, therefore nothing is wrong with you. You still feel terrible, though. Something *is* wrong with you. The doctor commits the **fallacy of ignorance**: the belief that not knowing something proves it doesn't exist.

It's always good to be skeptical of anything science hasn't proven. But, as a famous expression goes, absence of proof does not mean proof of absence. Science has not yet found intelligent life on other planets. Does that mean there are no smart and possibly furry aliens out there?

## *There's a first for every cat*

One of the many ways cats are smarter than humans is in cats' wise attitude toward antecedents. A cat will almost always be a little leery around a strange dog—even if that cat has met nothing but friendly dogs all his life. Now look at humans during rush hour. People who drive the same route every day without an accident tend to drive like lunatics. Why? They have been driving like lunatics on this same route for years, without a single accident! Therefore, nothing bad will ever happen, right? This fallacy, called the **fallacy of antecedent**, assumes that what happened before determines what happens after.

Before the Civil War, many Americans believed that the states would never fight each other. Why? Because they never had. A tragic fallacy of antecedent.

Now look at your average self-respecting cat. He sees you walk by with a plate of food, day after day, without ever letting him sample the food. Does that mean you will never give him a bite? No! That's a ridiculous fallacy and he will resist it by staring at you meaningfully every time you walk by. He will try different methods to persuade you to stop and let him have just a taste, or maybe a bite, or, if you're a true friend, all the meat on that plate. (You can have the vegetables.)

A cat knows there is a first for everything. And before every first, there was a long stretch of time when it hadn't happened yet.

People driving home from work on a Friday evening should think like wise cats. Many lives would be saved.

## *The tail-chasing fallacy*

Have you ever run across the word **tautology**? It's a kind of bad logic where the proof and the conclusion are the same.

For all their brains and good rhetoric, some cats get tautological on occasion.

Cat: I want to eat! [*Says this with a pitiful high mew.*]
You: Why? It's two hours before dinner.
Cat: Because I'm hungry. [*Says this with a pitiful high mew.*]

I want to eat, because I'm hungry. The conclusion (I want to eat) is pretty much the same as the proof (I'm hungry).

Another common cat tautology has to do with fun.

Cat: I want the tinsel stick! [*Says this by looking meaningfully toward the cupboard where the stick is kept.*]
You: Really? We just played with it an hour ago and I have chores to do. What on earth do you want the stick for now?
Cat: I want to play! [*Says this with a throaty meow and a meaningful look toward the cupboard.*]

Not all tautologies are this obvious. Some of the human ones—especially those manufactured by advertisers and politicians—can be hard to spot.

The cupcake diet lets you lose weight by shedding unwanted pounds!

Sure, you could shed *wanted* pounds by cutting off your own leg. Or, more reasonably, you could shed muscle. But "unwanted pounds" just means fat. And when most people think of losing weight, they imagine losing fat. So the cupcake diet lets you lose fat by shedding fat. That's a tautology. A cat would find it ridiculous. Unless the cupcake was made of tuna.

## *If it has claws, it's a fallacy*

Here's a very different kind of fallacy. It has to do with biting. When a cat tries to persuade you by biting your arm or clawing your leg, it's actually committing a fallacy named by Aristotle himself. Which, when you think about it, is pretty impressive. Aristotle called this kind of fallacy **argument by the stick**. Presumably he was not thinking about cats at the time. Otherwise he might have called it "argument by the claw."

What makes it a fallacy? A legitimate argument tries to convince someone to make a willing decision.

An argument by the stick therefore is not an argument but a fight. As you have seen, a successful argument makes an audience want to do something. Violence or a threat makes people do things unwillingly, under duress.

By the way: notice how we said "threat" as well as actual violence. Both count as the same fallacy, argument by the stick, because a threat can force people to do things they don't want to do, just as actual violence can. In other words, a hissing cat commits the same fallacy that a biting cat does, only less painfully.

# Biting is a last resort.

In rhetoric, violence is the only real fallacy.
Sure, a nip on the ankle can get you attention.
But a chomp ruins the conversation.

# 8. Talk with Your Body: The Eye Intrigue

*Convince with tone and gesture*

"The problem with cats is that they get the same exact look whether they see a moth or an ax murderer."

—Paula Poundstone

Cats understand that words are overrated. A cat's body language can really persuade. The same thing goes for us humans—even when it comes to persuading ourselves. For instance, good posture can fake confidence even when you're terrified speaking in front of a strange audience. Faking confidence can help you feel confident.

Then there are gestures—lifted chin, shrugged shoulder, obscene finger. Think of all the ways you can communicate without saying a word.

Not that we can ever be as silently articulate as a cat. Tragically, most of us humans lack a tail. And none of us will ever master the art of the Silent Meow.

But if we combine body language with words, we can upgrade our skills in arguing. Even with a cat.

Let's start with posture.

## *First, tuck in your tail*

Cats know that if you can keep a dignified, erect stance, you hardly need to exercise. Good posture makes you look fit. The trick is to stand and sit tall without any apparent effort—something cats do naturally. But then, cats have the advantage of four equal-sized limbs. Our arms-and-legs deal makes good posture harder for us, and so we need to work at it.

To stand like a leader, you should think of three key points: hips, shoulders and head.

1. Tuck in your hips so that your tail—that is, your rear end—doesn't stick out.
2. Pull your shoulders back, then let gravity relax them straight down towards your hips. One way to get there: Before you walk into a room, place your hands behind your head, barely touching the back of it. Pull your elbows back as far as you can. Hold this "surrender" pose for five seconds, relax and do it again.
3. Balance your head between your shoulders; you should be able to relax your neck completely without your head wandering anywhere.

Sitting works much the same way. It's just harder to sit straight than to stand straight. If you're alone on a recliner, reading or watching television, throw posture out of the window. Sit any way you want; this is a persuasion book, not a fitness book.

But suppose you're at a job interview, or appearing as a guest on *Jimmy Fallon*. The key to a great sitting posture is the head. Imagine your head as a balloon floating straight up toward the ceiling. Now let it pull your spine in the same direction. Keep that spine away from the back of the chair—it's a posture killer. To keep from looking stiff in this pose, relax your shoulders straight down—not forward, but down. Good. You're sitting like a cat.

Why go to all this bother?

A good posture makes you almost as respectable as a cat.

People will see you as a confident person. They may even ask if you've been working out. A good posture can give the appearance of losing 10 to 20 pounds. Sit properly while you have dessert.

What does that have to do with persuasion? A lot. Posture is the body-language version of basic grammar. It makes you seem well put-together. Like you know where you're coming from. With a good posture, like good grammar, you can hang out with the best of them.

Besides improving your image, posture can make you seem like a good listener. You're more likely to persuade if people think you're listening to their own opinions. Here's a great way to look as if you're listening even more than you are. (It does pay to really listen. It just pays even more to *show* that you are listening.) Start with the head. When someone else is talking, experiment with two ways of holding your head.

First, look straight into the speaker's eyes. Nod frequently—with little nods, not big ones. (Big, dramatic nodding implies you already know everything the person is saying. This is obnoxious.)

Now try looking down at the speaker's feet, still nodding slightly. This makes you seem as though you're listening intently. The first method is good if the speaker is telling a story or a joke. The second is best when the speaker is angry or upset; looking down makes you less threatening.

It's important to make this effort to look like you're listening. Cats do it by swiveling their ears. This is a much better listening technique. But most of us humans look ridiculous when we swivel our ears.

When you are the one doing the speaking, you need to do more than just stand straight. At the same time, try to keep your torso still. Here's a trick for when you speak to a group. Picture strapping a 20-pound iron ball to your waist. Imagine it dangling between your legs. Now think of keeping that ball from swinging. You do this by avoiding shifting your weight from leg to leg. And keep your feet still. This rock-solid stance makes your points seem rock solid. Pure confidence.

This imaginary weight trick works even if your audience is just one person, and even if you're sitting. Think of balancing right down your middle. This will help keep you from fidgeting or squirming. Your mother always told you not to fidget or squirm. And she was right. It distracts the listener.

For inspiration, watch a cat for an hour or two—especially a cat that's looking out the window at nothing in particular. An ear might move every now and then, just to show she's listening. Otherwise, monk-like, nothing-fazes-me stillness.

## *Now use your paws*

Once you have mastery over your body, it's time to think about your gestures. Because we lack a tail, most of our gestures have to be made with our arms and hands. This actually gives us an advantage over cats when we're shooting a video of ourselves. It's hard to see a cat's tail when he's talking. (Of course, cat videos will always be more popular, partly because they talk less than we do.)

You can express a lot just by crossing your arms. Avoid tucking your hands into your armpits. That signals defensiveness. It makes you look guilty or weak. Instead, grip around the outside of your upper arms—the biceps and triceps. This shows strength and self-respect.

In general, crossed arms communicate skepticism. They make you seem like a tough nut to crack. Cross your arms if someone is trying to talk you into doing something you don't want to do. But avoid this posture if you're the one trying to do the persuading.

Cats do not cross their arms to show self-respect or skepticism. Instead, they elegantly curl their tails. You will often see this gesture when you're trying to get a cat to do something he chooses not to do.

For humans, the opposite of crossed arms is the open-handed gesture. Use this when giving a talk. Stand with arms out as if you're ready to hug someone, palms facing the audience. This says: "I have trust in you, and have nothing to hide myself." Use the open-handed gesture at the end of a persuasive talk, when you're ready to let the audience make up its mind. In a one-to-one argument, this gesture says: "I don't want to fight; let's find a solution." It's great for dealing with an angry person. Or, at least, an angry person who isn't going to punch you while your arms are spread out.

The cat version of the open-handed gesture is a straight tail. When the tail sticks right out behind the cat, it signals trust as well as innocence. "Nobody is going to step on this," the tail says. "I feel perfectly safe around these big-footed humans." At the same time the cat is saying: "I have a clear conscience. I have not knocked anything off a shelf for at least 10 minutes."

Other hand gestures for us noncats:

Moving fists show power and aggression.
Twitching hands can signal humor, anger, or angry humor.
Circling hands show a kind of progress.
Moving both hands at once from side to side is a good way to imply "on the one hand . . ." kinds of points.

Most of the time, it's best to make the hands do the bulk of your gestures. Hold the rest of your body still. That's what cats do. Instead of moving hands they use a twitching tail. A cat who twitches just the tip of her tail may be ready to fight, either in play or for real. A cat that's getting ready to pounce—or at least considering the possibility of a pounce—will swing her whole tail from side to side.

Some cats wag their tails in pleasure, like a dog. It's important to know the difference between these gestures, so that you know when you're about to be pounced on, bitten or played with. Watching a human's hands can tell you the same thing.

When it comes to gestures, humans and cats aren't that different, really.

## *Finally, your beautiful eyes*

Cats know that the most persuasive facial expressions start with the eyes. Actually, cats start and end their expressions with the eyes. They understand what the great Roman orator and rhetorician Marcus Tullius Cicero said: "The eyes are the window to the soul."

To get people and cats to like and trust you, make sure you show the right kind of soul—that you're the kind who listens and empathizes, makes good choices and is overall a good sort of person. That's a lot of responsibility for the eyes to bear. But they're up to it.

Think in terms of *listening eyes* and *speaking eyes*. Listening eyes pay attention, and they think deeply about what the speaker is saying. To show you're paying the best attention in a one-on-one conversation, try this trick. Look into the eyeball—just one eyeball—of the speaker for a second or two, then switch your gaze to the other eyeball. Keep moving back and forth. This way you show deep attention, almost as if you're getting into the other person's head, without creepily staring. Try it. It works.

Speaking eyes lead the face in whatever emotion you're trying to express. If you're saying something humorous, try to smile only with your eyes. Direct all the energy in your face right to your eyes. Your listeners will see them "twinkle" or "sparkle"; that effect comes from the contractions of tiny muscles around your sockets, as well as the enlargement of your pupils.

Now try expressing sadness through your eyes. Let your brows and the rest of your face do their thing, but don't pay attention to anything but your eyes. Let them lead the way.

Look in a mirror, doing the humor and sadness eye thing. Experiment with other emotions: excitement, fear, anticipation, courage, love, anger. Again, channel all your energy into your eyes. With practice, you may find yourself expressing almost as well as a cat.

The face's other persuasive tool, of course, is the mouth. But this is a highly advanced, extremely sophisticated instrument. Yes, you can make it smile and frown, you can purse your lips or make them form a big surprised "O." But only a cat can perfect the epitome of mouth persuasion: the Silent Meow, or SM.

Even the finest actors in Hollywood—the human ones, that is—cannot match a cat's SM. It combines endearment and ingratiation with a special feline variety of hypnotism. You can learn a lot by studying this method, but don't expect to do it effectively yourself. It seems deceptively easy. While sitting gracefully on the floor, you gaze meaningfully up into the face of your victim. Now open your mouth as wide as you can—wider—and resume gazing. Repeat until your victim gives in to whatever you want (usually involves food or play, though you may have other needs).

Go on, try it. You will certainly fail to achieve anything but making a person laugh. Still, it's worth the experiment, if only to learn a valuable lesson: We will never come close to the persuasive ability of a cat.

# A silent meow trumps a loud one.

Eloquent silence, and a pathetic expression,
can persuade more than a shout.

# 9. Make Them Heed: The Lure and the Ramp

*Practice the greatest tools of persuasion*

"Never try to outstubborn a cat."
—Robert A. Heinlein

Now that you have learned the basics of rhetoric, it's time to get a person or a cat to do your bidding. So how can you get power over a cat?

Here's the secret: *Make the cat think she has the power.*

This technique works for humans as well. If you have a kid who is reluctant to get dressed, give her a choice of clothing. That makes her feel powerful.

Wrong: Would you please get dressed?
Right: Which do you want to wear, the red shirt or the blue one?

Offering a choice is a great way to make your audience feel powerful. Suppose you have a cat who only likes wet food. Lay out two different flavors of dry food and let her choose. Not only do the two flavors increase the chance that she will like one of them, but the act of choosing makes her feel in charge.

Another way to make a cat or a person feel powerful is to make her the hero of her own story. A cat who dislikes crunchy treats may eat them if they come in a ball with a small hole. When she rolls the ball around, a treat or two falls out, instantly becoming prey. Hiding food around the house can also increase the self-esteem of a picky cat. Every cat knows that food tastes much better when you kill it yourself. Humans do the same thing with video games and life goals. Hunting down a zombie or a goal makes the prize that much more delectable.

Here is one difference between cats and people: Humans can persuade themselves. Cats do not have to. They don't need goals, having accomplished them in a past life. And the biggest goal any soul can achieve is to earn the right to become a cat in the next one.

## *Pick a desire*

Getting a cat to do something you want it to do offers the same satisfaction and chance of success as, well, herding cats. But the philosopher Aristotle, who wrote the greatest book on persuasion ever, shows it is possible to move both cats and humans to action. You need two basic tools:

1. A lure.
2. A ramp.

The lure is all about desire. Without desire, it's hard to get any species to do anything it does not ordinarily want to do. To build desire, you need to create a lure. To a cat, a piece of chicken might make a suitable lure. To an adult male human, an attractive female will likely be an excellent lure. Or a piece of fried chicken.

Here's the interesting part: Just smelling a piece of fried chicken or seeing a beautiful woman makes a man more susceptible to buying a car. Lots of research proves this. To get a person or a cat to do something, you don't have to create desire for the action. You just have to create desire, period. Realtors will often suggest that you bake bread or heat some cinnamon in the oven before prospective buyers come over. The idea is to make the house seem more homey. But rhetoric and neuroscience say otherwise: The smell may just make people feel hungry, and when they're hungry, they're more likely to buy stuff. That's why, if you want to save money, you should eat before you go shopping, even shopping online.

You can increase your chances of persuading someone just by implanting a pleasant image in a human's head. Suppose you want a reluctant significant other to go on a cruise. Idly recall a beautiful sunny day, or a movie you both enjoyed. If you happen to be speaking before mealtime, mention a particularly great dinner you had together once. The pleasant thought need not have anything to do with cruising. You are changing the chemicals in the person's brain, making him more susceptible to saying yes. Consider this trick to be rhetorical chicken.

## *Look through the eyes of a cat*

People constantly make the mistake of arguing from their own point of view.

Parent: Why should I loan you the car?
Kid: Because I don't want to take the bus.

What's in it for the parent? Nothing.
People with cats commit the same rhetorical mistake when they argue with a cat over coming.

Jay: Killick, come!
Killick [*Using body language or possibly a word*]: Why?
Jay: You need to go to the vet.

Going to the vet is not a Good Thing. It may be necessary, and it may even be good for the cat in the long run, but the trip itself is a Bad Thing. Every cat knows this. Here are the Good Things that will make a cat come:

Food.
Play.
A toy.
A lap.

When you call a cat, you need to make it clear that a Good Thing is the outcome. Make sure you specify which Good Thing it is. A cat will use a different vocalization requesting food from one that urges you to play. You should offer him the same courtesy. Even in business, people will not call others to a meeting without saying what the meeting is about. When a cat is involved, the purpose of the meeting should be a Good Thing.

It's okay if you have an additional agenda, such as cleaning your cat's ears. Just make sure you provide the food, play, toy or lap first. And maybe after as well. Remember, failure to come through with the Good Thing is the same as a lie. This may sound extreme, and unique to cats, but it's not. A Good Thing is a kind of deal, and a deal is a promise, and a breach of promise is dishonest.

Besides, what's more important than the Good Things in life?

So, okay, you offer a piece of chicken. Now what? Suppose you want your cat to go willingly into the carrier box you use for trips to the vet. She knows that the box's only purpose is to transport her to a place full of barking smelly dogs where total strangers touch her and stick her with sharp things. The last thing any sensible cat will do is get in that awful box. Even the smallest cat can telescope her legs so that they're longer than the opening. Every cat, even a plump one, can defy physics and go two-dimensional, turning her body into an infinite flat plane. You need at least five hands, one for each leg and one for the body, to origami the cat into a shape that fits into the box.

Or you can somehow make the cat want to enter the box. Willingly. Of her own accord.

## *Turn a leap into a ramp*

For most cats, just putting a piece of chicken into the box is not a sufficient lure. But if you put a series of pieces on the floor, with the last, juiciest one in the box itself, you stand a chance. Each piece acts as an appetizer for the next one.

The human version of this technique is to build tiny steps into your goal. Suppose you're job hunting. You find a company with a suitable opening, send in your résumé, and—predictably—nothing happens. Sending your résumé is the same as putting a piece of chicken in the carrier box. The résumé may build the employer's desire. After all, you're the perfect candidate! But yours is buried in a stack of other résumés.

You need more chicken pieces that lead the way to your résumé. Appetizers, if you will. So you make sure that the employer sees you on LinkedIn and Twitter. You attend a workshop taught by someone in the company. You make yourself visible in bits, like chicken. And you build desire gradually.

But desire is not enough. The cat might not take the chicken after all. She might just vacuum up the trail right up to the carrier box and then sit and clean her face. "I'm done," says her body language.

What went wrong? Aristotle himself said that to get someone to take an action you need to build desire. He encouraged every speaker to talk eloquently about the outcome of the decision you want, building desire for that goal. Modern neuroscience shows that building desire for just about anything, putting someone in a hungry or lustful mood, can create all the desire you need in an audience. This is beneficial, since speaking eloquently to a cat rarely works. Only humans are dumb enough to fall for that. But even cats will succumb to a feeling of need, one that can be created just by opening a can of tuna.

And still that might not be enough. How do you get the cat into the carrier box? How do you get a distracted employer actually to hire you?

You need a ramp.

## *Make it seem effortless*

Aristotle didn't talk about ramps. Instead, he said that, besides building desire for a goal, you need to do something else: *Make the action seem easy.*

But what if the thing you want is actually kind of hard? Such as going to the trouble of hiring you over every other candidate? Or, even harder, getting your cat to walk into the dreaded carrier box?

Let's deal with the box first. If you can get the cat to walk willingly into a carrier box, you can get a human to do just about anything. And here's where the ramp comes in. Try this.

Take a 6-foot-long board of almost any width. Nail strips crosswise every 6 inches. Now take the carrier box and place it high up on a counter. Arrange it so that the rest of the counter is blocked off. Lean the board against the counter so that it leads right up to the entrance of the box. You can put pieces of chicken on the strips, but you may not have to. Most cats find it hard to resist a ramp. Like humans, they want to ascend in the world. Do put a treat in the box itself, if only as a reward. Chances are, the cat will explore the ramp. Each step up is an itty-bitty action, making each next step seem easier. The box itself is just another step, not some big commitment. What's more, the ramp—the series of small ascending steps—transforms the box from a nasty place to something that seems inevitable, even desirable: the highest part of the ramp.

## *Break it into chunks*

How does the ramp technique work on humans? To get a person to do something hard, break it down into small, easy steps. Offer a reward or praise at each little step.

A great way to try out the ramp technique is to use it on yourself. Suppose you want to get in shape for the summer. The very idea of dieting and working out exhausts you. Instead, think of the easiest possible first step. The biggest problem people have with exercising is finding the time. Spend two weeks going to bed five minutes earlier and setting your alarm five minutes earlier, until you have essentially put yourself into another time zone. Don't even try to exercise during this period. Just build the time. One little step. Then begin exercising for 10 minutes each week-day, and gradually increase the amount over two months until you get to half an hour or more. Eventually you'll acquire a first-class exercise habit.

What about food? Same thing. Instead of dieting, start by writing down everything you eat. Just write it down. Don't calculate calories, and eat your usual food in the usual portions. After a week, start counting the calories. Again, don't change what you eat, just record it. The next week, change one thing: the portion sizes in one meal, or swap a soda for a cup of tea. Each week that follows, change one more thing.

Once you've mastered the ramp for self-persuasion, you can use it to persuade someone else. Suppose you want to sell a chair at a yard sale. Don't ask people to buy it. Ask them to sit in it.

Or, back to our job hunt: Ask prospective employers for an informational interview rather than a job. Tell each person that you want to know how he became so success-ful in his profession. It's the equivalent of placing a piece of chicken on a ramp. Most people are glad to talk about their successes. After he does, ask him for other contacts, and say you would like to keep in touch. That leads him a bit further up the ramp. When the time is ripe, you use him to help you get hired. Turn your new contact into your cat ramp.

While history does not record whether Aristotle had cats, he certainly knew how to persuade them. Build desire, then set up a ramp. Make the goal as tempting as possible, then coax your audience to take a tiny step toward that goal. First try it with a cat and a carrier box. Then use the lure-and-ramp technique to make humans do your bidding.

If you succeed, you can conquer the world.

# Sniff it first.

Beware of lures that make you do things you don't want. If something looks tasty, take a gander. Then walk away. Then come back and sniff it. Then eat. You will regret fewer things. And probably lose weight.

# 10. Follow the Steps:
# The Cat Persuasion Checklist

*Make sure you've dotted the rhetorical "i"s*

> "Cats know how to obtain food without labour,
> shelter without confinement, and love
> without penalties."
> —Walter Lionel George

This checklist works for both cats and humans. Go through it before you attempt any serious persuasion.

## What's your goal?

Too often when we get into a disagreement with a loved one—pet or otherwise—we try to dominate the other person. Or we back off, out of reach from any claws. Instead, ask yourself whether the relationship is more important than the argument. Or, if you want something (a cat on your lap, a new car), work on getting that. It may be better to make your opponent feel like he won even while you end up getting what you want.

## Is this a good time to persuade?

A persuader seizes every opportunity. The perfect time to get a cat to come is when he is hungry. The best time to persuade a man of *anything* is when he is hungry.

## What mood is your opponent in?

If this seems like a bad time, you can make it a good one by changing your audience's mood (see page 47). Make it feel powerful, comfortable and (if it's a human) make it smile.

## Is he paying attention?

A distracted audience is much harder to persuade. When you argue with your cat, you must entertain him.

## What tense are you using?

Angry people usually use the past tense ("Look what you did!") or the present tense ("Bad cat!"). If you want to get your audience to change its mind or do something, try switching to the future tense ("Come here and I'll give you a treat").

## Are you loving your audience, or pretending to?

If your audience is a cat, then loving it should be easy. It's sometimes harder with people. But if you pretend to enjoy their company, you may find yourself actually enjoying it. At any rate, they will like you more.

## Does he like and trust you?

Ethos (see page 54) is persuasion's most powerful tool. It is the image your cat has of you. Does he find you reliable? Do you provide the best of all laps? Then he is much more likely to come when you call. And possibly less likely to knock the pen off your desk. Unless he thinks that, from the kindness of your heart, you put the pen there for him.

## Does your argument make sense to your audience?

In persuasion, facts and statistics aren't terribly important to a cat. Or to most people, for that matter. Instead, focus on what your audience believes and expects. That does not mean lying. But your audience will not mind if you pretend that a red laser dot is an alien space bug that must be killed.

## Is your posture good?

See Chapter 8. As every cat knows, a dignified posture wins respect.

## Do you look confident?

Part of good posture is good self-attitude, even if you're faking it. And faking confidence can make it real. Don't think of the times you missed. Think about all your successful kills.

### Have you broken up the action into chunks?

Chapter 9 talks about the lure and the ramp. Ask your audience to do a little thing, and then another little thing, eventually leading to a big action. That's ramping. When you want action, ask for bits of action. And offer little bits of treat each step of the way.

# A dead mouse is a trophy.

Do not wait for others to celebrate your accomplishments. When you kill something, leave it on someone's bed.

# Epilogue: Cats of Character

*And what they've taught us*

"What greater gift than the love of a cat."
Charles Dickens

The cats in our lives have all been great friends and worthy opponents.

**Sassy**, jet black and decisive, was the alpha male when Jay was growing up. Sassy did not suffer fools. He considered Jay one of them. This cat was the commanding sort of arguer who often got his way through threats—hissing and an occasional swipe. Mostly, he was decisive. Knowing what you want is the first rule of persuasion.

**Willow**, an abandoned kitten, talked Jay's little brother into taking her home. Then she used her skills on a reluctant dad. It helped that she was adorable: a perfect light grey, like pussy willow.

**Zelmo** was a street cat in Washington, DC. He was what the French call a *flâneur*, a man about town. Zelmo assumed everyone loved him, and so they did. We all should be more like Zelmo. Assume you are loved, and most people will love you.

A few days before Christmas, somebody placed **Charlie** in a box with his brother, Percy. The box got left at a police station. Charlie adopted Natalie's 11-year-old daughter, Amelie. He sleeps on a bookshelf in her room and converses loudly with her. Good conversationalists are rare, especially among cats. Amelie writes about Charlie: "A playful, curious cat who is hungry for adventure (and mice), he is loving and smart and cute. He is also my alarm clock. He acts as my bodyguard, sitting at the bottom of my stairs. We are so attached to each other and we look after each other. When it comes to food he is very sneaky as you can see his paw gradually getting closer to your plate and then he strikes and misses."

**Percy**, Charlie's brother, adopted Amelie's 9-year-old brother, Ben. We'll let Ben take over here: "Percy is a loving cat who always follows the person he loves the most. He never stops purring. He is loyal and able to find his owner wherever he is. He is very stinky and has a mini beard on his chin. He loves to be cuddled and stroked but if you want to cuddle him, you have to approach him in the right way." This is true of humans as well. Percy died young, which is very sad.

After Percy came **Dottie**, the world's most agreeable cat. Knowing that agreeability is the most persuasive attitude of all, Dottie uses her love of everybody to get everything she wants. Whenever Charlie grooms himself, she lies right under his tongue to get a free bath. Whenever Charlie lies down for a nap, she uses him for a pillow. And Charlie never complains, because Dottie is so agreeable. She even practices decorum: With impeccable table manners, she sits quietly until people stop paying her attention. Then she steals their food.

**Isabella** came along when Jay's young daughter began hanging up cat calendars. (You can see more of Isabella in a little book he published on Blurb.com, *Sniff It First, & 15 Other Things I Learned From My Cat*.) Isabella was territorial, ill-behaved and rather fat. But she knew how to be funny. With a good sense of slapstick you will go far in this world.

Bat-eared, great-souled **Aubrey** was born with many physical problems. Though he couldn't walk properly, he gently ruled over his much larger brother, **Maturin**. Aubrey lived less than two years. But the greatest persuasion is the way you live your life. Aubrey was the best of all persuaders.

**Killick** was bred as an Italian stud. Though he has been fixed, he still acts like a stud. The world exists to entertain him. This belief makes him an entertaining companion. Great persuaders know that, in order to persuade, they must hold their audience's attention. Give Killick a paper clip or a shoelace (especially one you're attempting to tie) and he will turn it into a circus.

**Dorothy Jr** and **George** (daughter and son of Jay) and **Amelie** and **Ben** (daughter and son of Natalie) are technically human. But they are all charming and loyal and as hard to persuade as cats. We love them all.

Small persuasive creatures rule
the world.

# About the Author

Jay Heinrichs is the bestselling author of *Thank You for Arguing*. He has written for dozens of publications, including *The New York Times Magazine*, *Vice* and the *Huffington Post*, and won numerous journalism awards. He has taught persuasion to editors at Ivy League universities, NASA and the Pentagon. He runs the acclaimed blog Figarospeech.com, as well as the rhetoric site ArgueLab.com.

jayheinrichs.com

Available from *New York Times* bestselling author

# JAY HEINRICHS

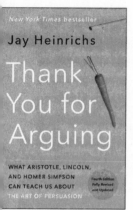

"Cross Cicero with
David Letterman and you
get Jay Heinrichs."

—JOSEPH ELLIS, Pulitzer Prize-winning author
of *Founding Brothers* and *American Sphinx*